BOY SCOUTS OF AMERICA
MERIT BADGE SERIES

DISABILITIES AWARENESS

BOY SCOUTS OF AMERICA.

Requirements

1. Discuss with your counselor proper disability etiquette and person-first language. Explain why these are important.

2. Visit an agency that works with people with physical, mental, emotional, or educational disabilities. Collect and read information about the agency's activities. Learn about opportunities its members have for training, employment, and education.

3. Do TWO of the following:

    a. Talk to a Scout who has a disability and learn about his experiences taking part in Scouting activities and earning different merit badges.

    b. Talk to an individual who has a disability and learn about this person's experiences and the activities in which this person likes to participate.

    c. Learn how people with disabilities take part in a particular adaptive sport or recreational activity. Discuss what you have learned with your counselor.

    d. Learn about independent living aids such as service animals, canes, and teletypewriters (TTYs). Discuss with your counselor how people use such aids.

4. Visit TWO of the following locations and take notes about the accessibility to people with disabilities. In your notes, give examples of five things that could be done to improve upon the site and five things about the site that make it friendly to people with disabilities. Discuss your observations with your counselor.

    a. Your school

    b. Your place of worship

    c. Your Scout camping site

    d. A public exhibit or attraction (such as a theater, museum, or park)

5. Explain what advocacy is. Do ONE of the following advocacy activities:

    a. Present a counselor-approved disabilities awareness program to a Cub Scout pack or other group. During your presentation, explain and use person-first language.

    b. Find out about disability awareness education programs in your school or school system, or contact a disability advocacy agency. Volunteer with a program or agency for eight hours.

    c. Using resources such as disability advocacy agencies, government agencies, the Internet (with your parent's permission), and news magazines, learn about myths and misconceptions that influence the general public's understanding of people with disabilities. List 10 myths and misconceptions about people with disabilities and learn the facts about each myth. Share your list with your counselor, then use it to make a presentation to a Cub Scout pack or other group.

6. Make a commitment to your merit badge counselor describing what you will do to show a positive attitude about people with disabilities and to encourage positive attitudes among others. Discuss how your awareness has changed as a result of what you have learned.

7. Name five professions that provide services to people with disabilities. Pick one that interests you and find out the education, training, and experience required for this profession. Discuss what you learn with your counselor, and tell why this profession interests you.

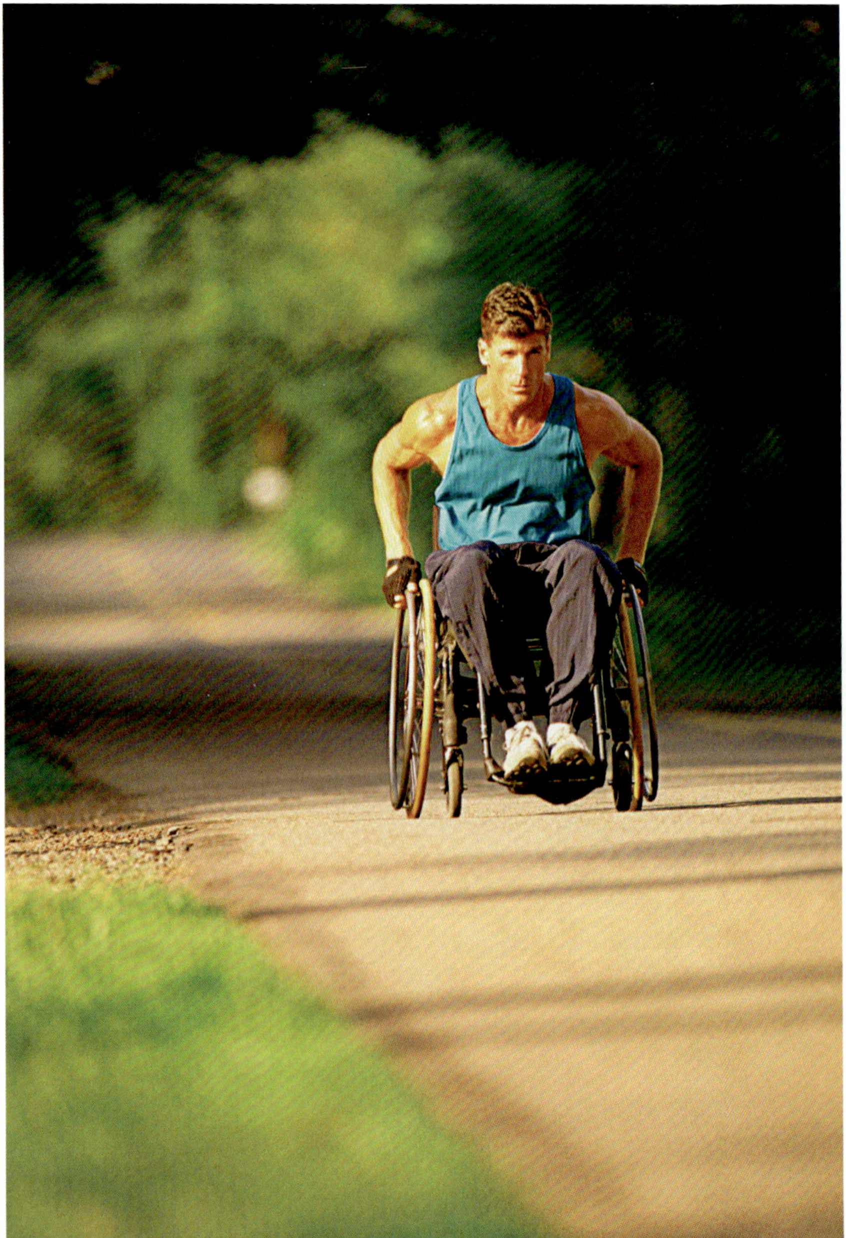

Contents

People First 7

Agencies 15

Activities and Adaptations 19

Accessibility 33

Advocacy, Attitudes, and Awareness 39

Career Opportunities 49

Disabilities Awareness Resources 54

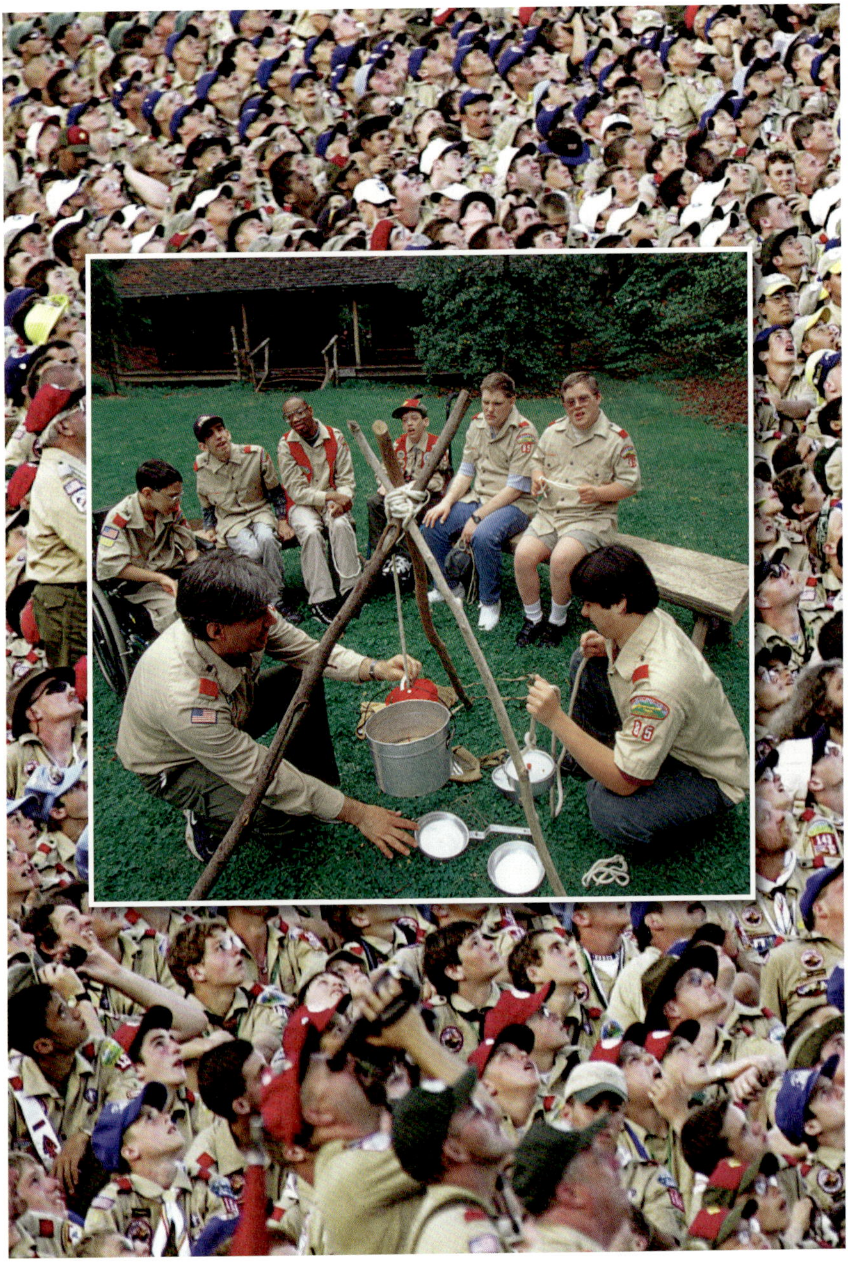

People First

Look around at the Scouts in your unit, the members of your sports teams, and the kids in your class. You are not all alike, are you?

Your friends, teammates, and classmates have separate personalities, distinct interests and ideas, and different physical features. You do not all look alike, think alike, or act alike. You have your own skills and strengths, and your own needs and situations.

> "Beware, as long as you live, of judging people by appearances."
> —Jean de La Fontaine (1621–95), French poet

People who have disabilities are no different from the members of your group or any other group of individuals. A person might use a wheelchair or be deaf or hard of hearing. A friend from school might be a terrible speller. Your Scout patrol leader might dislike heights.

You know there is more to your patrol leader than his aversion to high places. You know your friend does many things well, even if he has a hard time spelling. In the same way, people who have disabilities are not defined by their disabilities. A person might have hearing loss, wear leg braces, or have a medical condition such as epilepsy, but that's not who he or she is.

PEOPLE FIRST

Disability Etiquette

When you meet someone who has a disability, that might be the first thing you notice. Because the person *seems* different, you might be a little uncomfortable or even scared at first.

Just remember that the disability is not the person. Look beyond the wheelchair, crutches, leg braces, hearing aid, or whatever seems different. See the person and treat him or her as an individual—the way you like to be treated.

Here are some tips for disability etiquette.

The disability is not the person.

1. When you meet someone who has a disability, it is always appropriate to smile and say hello. You also may offer to shake hands (shaking hands with the left hand is OK). While people with artificial limbs or limited use of their hands do shake hands, remember that not everyone can. When in doubt, ask the person whether he or she would like to shake hands with you.

2. When you talk with someone who uses a wheelchair, sit down so you will be at eye level with the wheelchair user. This is not only polite, but it shows the same level of respect with which you like to be treated.

3. Do not lean on a person's wheelchair.

DISABILITIES AWARENESS

4. Do not touch or move a person's wheelchair, crutches, cane, or other gear without permission.

5. If a sign-language interpreter helps you talk with a person who is deaf, look at and speak to the person, not the interpreter. In fact, any time you talk with a person who has a disability, speak directly to that person rather than to any companion who may be along.

6. Be patient if a person with a disability takes a little extra time to do or say something.

7. When you talk with someone who has difficulty speaking, never pretend to understand if you do not. If you don't catch what was said, ask the speaker to repeat it. Then tell the speaker what you understood. The person will correct or clarify things if necessary.

8. Speak in a normal voice. Do not shout. Shouting hinders lipreading and distorts the sounds that hearing aids pick up. Obviously, it does not help to shout at people who are blind or visually impaired. They might not see you, but they can hear you.

9. Never pet or play with service animals such as guide dogs. Service animals are working animals, not pets, and should not be distracted from their duties.

10. Ask before giving help. If the person accepts your offer of help, wait for instructions or ask how you can help.

11. Offer your arm to a person who has a visual impairment, or suggest that the person put a hand on your shoulder. This will let you guide, rather than push or pull, the person as you walk together. Give warning of doors, stairs, or curbs as you approach them.

12. When talking with someone who is deaf or hard of hearing, first get the person's attention with a light tap on the shoulder, or wave your hand or stand in front of the person and make eye contact before you speak. If the person lip-reads, face him or her directly. Speak clearly and not too fast. Let the person choose the means of communication, such as lipreading, sign language, or writing notes.

Ask your parents or adult leaders not to park in places reserved for people with disabilities. People need the large parking spaces to maneuver wheelchairs, wheelchair lifts, and other mobility equipment.

13. When talking with someone who is blind, identify yourself and anyone with you by name. When you are ending the conversation or getting ready to leave, let the person know. Don't just walk away.

14. Relax and be yourself. It is fine and natural to use common expressions such as "Did you hear about . . . ?" or "See you later" or "Got to run." Everyday language does not offend people who are deaf or blind or use wheelchairs, and is understandable to most people with mental disabilities. Picking your words with too much care will make everyone self-conscious and uncomfortable.

15. If you want to know about someone's disability, it is OK to ask, politely. It is also OK for the person not to talk about it.

16. Treat people with friendship and respect. A Scout is courteous. Show courtesy to all people, those with and those without disabilities.

Who Are People With Disabilities?

David Larson, wheelchair-racing champion, competitor in three Paralympic Games, and world record–holder for the 400-meter race, was diagnosed with cerebral palsy at age 2.

Chris Waddell, champion mono-skier and winner of numerous gold and silver medals in the Paralympics and world championships, was paralyzed below the waist in a skiing accident when he was 20.

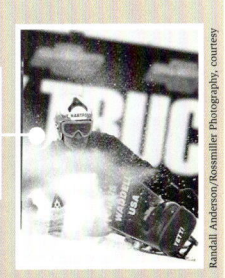

Danny Glover, star of films such as "The Color Purple" and the "Lethal Weapon" series, is a full-time activist for such causes as anemia awareness, the AIDS crisis in Africa, and math education in the United States. He has dyslexia.

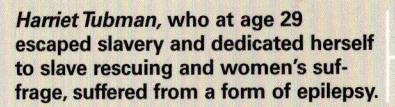

Harriet Tubman, who at age 29 escaped slavery and dedicated herself to slave rescuing and women's suffrage, suffered from a form of epilepsy.

James E. West, successful attorney and the first Chief Scout Executive of the Boy Scouts of America, had a disease in one leg that gave him a permanent physical disability.

Wilma Mankiller, the first woman to hold the position of principal chief of the Cherokee Nation, was diagnosed with a rare form of muscular dystrophy.

Franklin D. Roosevelt, who served as president of the United States longer than any other president, used a wheelchair most of his life after nearly dying from polio.

Person-First Language

People with disabilities are *people* first. The idea behind *person-first language* is to emphasize the person, not the disability.

Don't call someone an epileptic when you mean to say the person has epilepsy. The condition and the person are not one and the same. For example, when describing someone who has autism, you would say "this child has autism," not "this child is autistic." The condition does not define the child.

Try to always put the person first when you talk or write about people who have disabilities. This is an easy habit to develop. Use this list of terms to help you get the person-first habit.

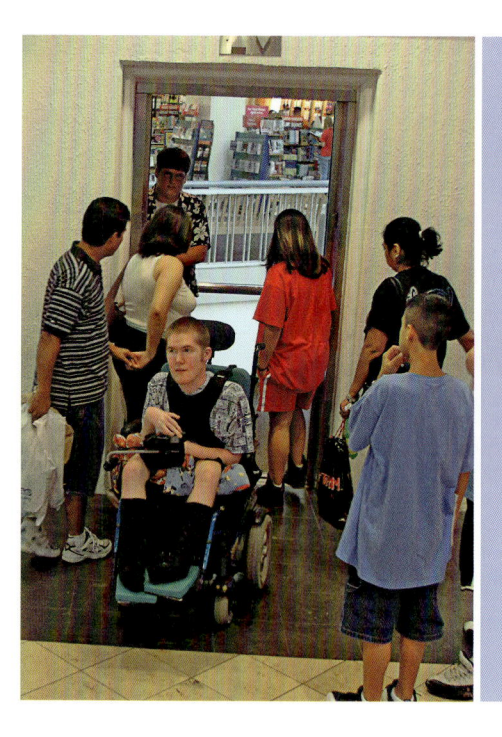

A *disability* is a condition that may limit a person's mobility, hearing, vision, speech, or mental function. A *handicap* is a restriction or a disadvantage that is placed on a person. For example, some people with disabilities use wheelchairs. Stairs, curbs, and narrow doors are handicaps that hinder people who use wheelchairs. People with disabilities are not "handicapped" unless these kinds of barriers are put in their way.

Say	Instead of
Person with a disability	Disabled person
People with disabilities	The disabled or the handicapped
Disability	Handicap
Person who has epilepsy, autism, a spinal cord injury, etc.	An epileptic, an autistic, a quadriplegic, etc. (Never identify people only by their disability. A person is not a condition.)
Seizure	Fit
Person who is deaf or hard of hearing	Hearing-impaired person ("Hard of hearing" is preferred to "hearing-impaired," which translates in sign language as "broken hearing.")
Person with Down syndrome	A Down's person
Has a mental or developmental disability	Is retarded or slow
Has had a disability since birth, or was born with a disability	Has a birth defect
Wheelchair user/person who uses a wheelchair, or person who uses or walks with crutches	Confined/restricted to a wheelchair; wheelchair-bound (People use wheelchairs and crutches for getting around. Most people who use such devices see them as liberating, not confining.)
People without disabilities/nondisabled	Healthy, normal, able-bodied (Calling people who are not disabled "healthy" suggests that people with disabilities are unhealthy. In fact, many people who have disabilities are in excellent health. Similarly, labeling nondisabled people as "normal" incorrectly implies that people who have disabilities are "abnormal.")
Accessible parking/ accessible restrooms	Handicapped parking/ handicapped restrooms

THE ARC OF DALLAS
Making life better for people
with developmental disabilities since 1951.

Agencies

To fulfill requirement 2 for the Disabilities Awareness merit badge, you will visit an agency that serves people who have physical, mental, emotional, or learning disabilities. Work with your merit badge counselor to choose an appropriate agency or organization and make an appointment to visit.

> **Tip:** Many national organizations have state and regional affiliates, as well as local chapters. To find a chapter near you, look in the white pages of your local phone book, or (with your parent's permission) check the agency's Web site. Also see the resources section of this pamphlet.

Be prepared to ask questions during your visit. Find out about the services provided.

Depending on the agency, the services offered might include the following:

- *Physical therapy* to develop or restore movement, strength, or flexibility lost because of an injury, an illness, or a physical condition

Agencies

Many agencies are available to help people with temporary or permanent disabilities.

- *Speech-hearing therapy* to improve or recover limited or lost communication skills, treat disabilities such as language delay and stuttering, and teach other ways of communication to people who are unable to speak or hear
- *Occupational therapy* to develop the ability and independence to do everyday activities such as bathing, dressing, and eating
- *Educational programs* matched to students' ages, needs, and abilities
- *Skills training* to build skills that people need at work
- *Employment services* to help people find the kinds of positions they want

The agency or organization also might sponsor camps, arts and crafts, recreation programs, or sports teams for young people with disabilities. Perhaps you can talk with someone your age who has taken part in recreational programs or received services.

Take home any brochures or fliers from your visit. Read the material. Then discuss with your counselor what you learned about the agency, its activities, and the people it serves.

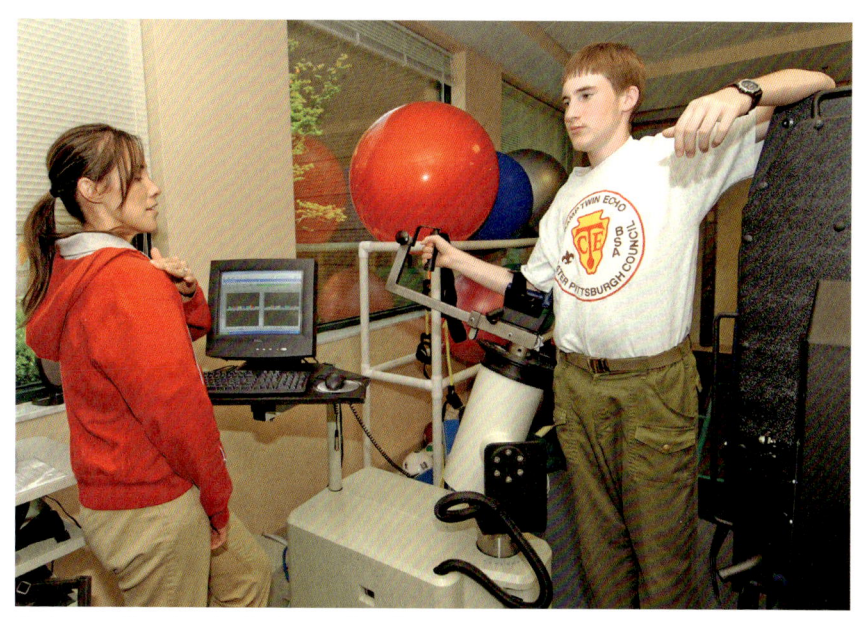

Understanding the physical struggles of a person who has a disability may help you recognize the individual's unique challenges.

Guide dogs are trained to safely lead their owners anywhere they need to go.

Activities and Adaptations

In your personal or patrol camping gear, you have tents, cook kits, backpacking stoves, sleeping bags, and other tools that help you live well and be self-sufficient in the outdoors. People with various types of disabilities use various types of tools to be comfortable and self-sufficient at home, at school, at work, during leisure time, and while traveling.

Tools for independent living may be as basic as a variable-height table that a wheelchair user can adjust to fit. Tools can be as simple and commonsense as lights that flash when the doorbell rings to let a person who is deaf know someone is at the door.

Other tools are more high-tech. People who cannot use their hands, for example, to type on a keyboard or move a computer mouse, can operate computers by talking. Voice-recognition software lets users speak commands to call up programs, dictate documents, write e-mails, move the cursor on the screen, navigate online, and create Web pages.

Here are some other tools and supports that can help people with disabilities do the things they want and need to accomplish.

ACTIVITIES AND ADAPTATIONS

Service Animals

Guide dogs can help people who are blind get around safely, quickly, and with confidence. A guide dog responds to its owner's hand signals and spoken commands. The main commands spoken to a guide dog are "forward," "left," "right," "hop up," "halt," and "steady." A guide dog is trained to disobey a command that might put its owner in danger. If the owner gives the command "forward," but the dog sees an obstacle in the way, such as a car, the dog will refuse to move forward.

People who are deaf or hard of hearing may have *hearing dogs* to alert them to important sounds: a ringing telephone, a knock at the door, an alarm clock buzzing, or a noise that might mean danger. A hearing dog will lead its owner to most sounds. But at the shriek of a smoke alarm, the dog is trained to take its owner to the nearest exit.

Assistance dogs can help people with physical or developmental disabilities do everyday tasks. Assistance dogs can open and close doors and drawers, flip light switches on and off, retrieve dropped items, and bring or carry objects such as keys, coins, mail, books, a phone, or a water bottle. An assistance dog can be trained to make its body rigid so its owner can brace against the dog when standing up. If the owner uses a wheelchair, the dog may pull the wheelchair short distances while the owner holds onto the dog's harness.

DISABILITIES AWARENESS

Assistance dogs are trained to perform everyday tasks for their owners.

Capuchin or "organ grinder" monkeys are smart, friendly, nimble-fingered, and particularly well-suited to be trained as *monkey helpers*. They can help people with many kinds of daily activities: opening doors, holding pencils, operating switches, fetching out-of-reach items, bringing a cool drink, turning the pages of a book, or putting on a video or CD to play. Monkey assistants can even be office workers, helping people with quadriplegia (paralysis of both arms and both legs) do work from their homes.

People who have epilepsy may rely on *seizure response dogs* to live on their own and get help in an emergency. A seizure response dog is trained to run back and forth from its owner to someone who can help, getting the second person's attention and repeating the alert signal as long as needed. If the dog is alone with its owner, the dog can pull a cord on a call box to bring emergency medical personnel. The dog stays with its owner until the seizure ends or help arrives.

ACTIVITIES AND ADAPTATIONS

Touching Words: The Braille Alphabet

Braille is a system of printing and writing that uses raised points or dots. In Braille, each letter, number, and punctuation mark is made up of one to six raised dots arranged in a "cell." The cell, two dots wide and three dots high, fits under a fingertip. People read Braille by lightly passing their fingers over the dots.

The Braille alphabet is shown here. Notice that the first 10 letters *(a–j)* use only the dots in the upper two rows of the cell. The next 10 letters *(k–t)* are formed by adding the lower-left dot to each of the first 10 letters. The remaining letters *(except w)* are formed by adding both lower dots to each of the first five letters.

The letter *w* is an exception because the French alphabet did not contain a *w* when French inventor Louis Braille created the code in the 1820s. The symbol for *w* was added later.

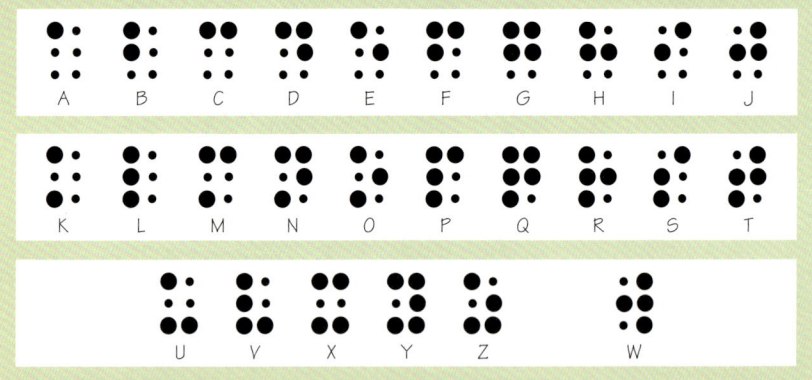

The Braille alphabet

Braille can be written by hand using a slate and stylus, or typed by striking keys on a machine resembling a typewriter, called a braillewriter. Today, there are software programs that translate Braille; computer printers that emboss Braille dots on thick, heavy paper; portable, electronic note takers with Braille keyboards and synthesized voice readouts; and Braille displays that make the characters on a computer screen appear on a touchable surface.

22 DISABILITIES AWARENESS

ACTIVITIES AND ADAPTATIONS

White Canes

The white cane is both a tool for travel and a symbol telling others that the person using the cane is blind. The white cane makes blind pedestrians more visible to motorists, helping them travel in greater safety.

By tapping the cane from side to side in front of them as they walk, people who are blind or visually impaired can check for objects in the path of travel, find doorways and steps, and locate potential dangers such as holes in the sidewalk or curbs and drop-offs.

Power Chairs

Modern battery-powered wheelchairs hardly resemble the push-from-behind type of wheelchair you may have seen used in hospitals. Most power chairs have a variable speed control that can be set between 0 and a top speed of about 5 miles per hour. With a fully charged battery, most power chairs will travel between 15 and 20 miles on level surfaces. Some power chairs break down into sections to fit in the trunk of a car for transport.

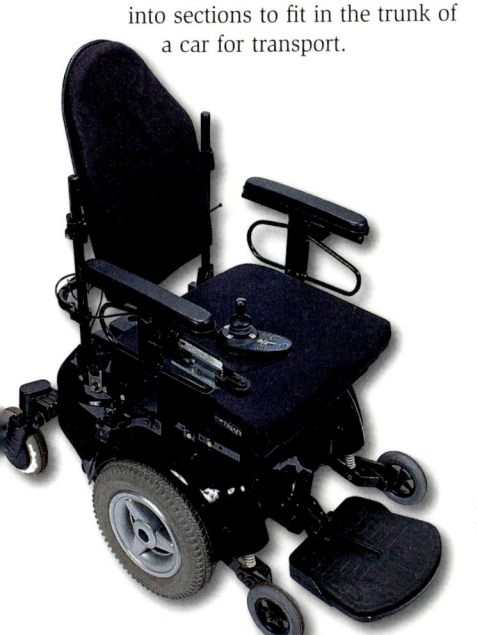

It takes much practice to learn how to skillfully use a cane to avoid obstacles and travel independently.

A modern power wheelchair

DISABILITIES AWARENESS 23

ACTIVITIES AND ADAPTATIONS

Teletypewriters

Teletypewriters (TTYs), also called telecommunication devices for the deaf (TDDs), enable people who are deaf or hard of hearing to communicate by telephone. TTYs have keyboards for entering messages and monitors that display the conversation as users type back and forth. Users communicate in real time, similar to instant messaging by computer.

Today, many people who are deaf or hard of hearing use wireless messaging systems that let the user send and receive e-mail, TTY messages, faxes, and text-to-speech/speech-to-text messages. Relay services also make it possible for hearing people to communicate by telephone with deaf or hard-of-hearing persons. Relay operators receive calls, speak the typed portion of the call to the hearing person, and type the spoken part of the conversation to the TTY user.

Teletypewriter

Video Relay Service

Video relay service (VRS) is a new Internet video service that lets a person who uses sign language place a call to a hearing person (or vice versa), with a sign-language interpreter relaying the conversation. VRS allows people to sign rather than type their messages. Most people who are fluent in sign language find signing much faster than pounding a keyboard. Also, communications are clearer because people can use facial expressions and gestures to help get their message across.

24   DISABILITIES AWARENESS

===== ACTIVITIES AND ADAPTATIONS

Here is how VRS works:

- The person who uses sign language needs a videophone or a webcam and a high-speed Internet connection. A hearing person needs only a standard telephone.

- A call is placed to the relay operator, also known as a video interpreter or communication assistant. The operator connects the two parties—the nonhearing person and the hearing person.

- The nonhearing person uses sign language, the hearing person speaks, and they carry on a conversation through the relay operator, who communicates by speaking to the hearing person and by signing via video to the nonhearing person.

Finger Spelling

Many people who are deaf learn to finger spell by using hand shapes and positions that stand for the letters of the written alphabet. Finger spelling is like writing in air. Shown here is the American Manual Alphabet. Try using this alphabet to spell out your name.

The American Manual Alphabet used for finger spelling

DISABILITIES AWARENESS 25

ACTIVITIES AND ADAPTATIONS

Adaptive Sports

Many people with disabilities use adaptive equipment to take part in sports and recreational activities. Any sport can be an adaptive sport. Among the most popular are:

- Adaptive golf
- Adaptive snow skiing
- Adaptive water skiing
- Archery
- Beep baseball
- Bocce
- Canoeing
- Goal ball
- Handcycling
- Horseback riding
- Kayaking
- Power wheelchair hockey
- Quad rugby
- Sailing
- Sitting volleyball
- Sledge hockey
- Snowboarding
- Swimming
- Wheelchair basketball
- Wheelchair football
- Wheelchair road racing
- Wheelchair soccer
- Wheelchair softball
- Wheelchair tennis
- Wheelchair track and field
- Whitewater rafting

ACTIVITIES AND ADAPTATIONS

Sports may need a few modifications to be accessible to people with disabilities. Canoeists with disabilities, for example, may use seats that give extra back support and paddles with modified shafts and grips. Wheelchair archers commonly use the same archery tackle as standing archers. An armrest of the wheelchair may be removed to allow the archer to fully draw the bowstring.

Custom equipment opens other popular sports to people who have disabilities. Adaptive snow-skiing gear includes the bi-ski (two skis with a molded bucket seat for the skier to sit in), mono-ski (a one-ski type of sit-down ski), four-track (stand-up skiing using two skis with two handheld outriggers for balance, giving the skier four points of contact with the snow), and three-track (stand-up skiing with one ski and two handheld outriggers).

DISABILITIES AWARENESS 27

Activities and Adaptations

Handcycling is among the newer sports popular with athletes who have disabilities. Three-wheeled handcycles have gears like bicycles, and riding one is much like riding a bike except you power the cycle by cranking with your arms and upper body muscles instead of your legs. Recreational handcyclists typically cruise along as fast as an average bicyclist. Handcycle racers are setting human-powered vehicle speed records.

To find out what adaptive sports and recreation activities are available in your community, contact the parks and recreation department, school athletic department, rehabilitation centers, or sporting goods stores that sell adaptive sports equipment. To learn more about your sport of interest, you may be able to attend an introductory clinic, seminar, or demo day given by an adaptive sports organization.

ACTIVITIES AND ADAPTATIONS

Can You Adapt?

Test your creativity. Choose one of your favorite activities and think of ways you could adapt it so people with various types of disabilities could enjoy it, too. Will you need to modify the rules? The rules of wheelchair basketball, for instance, allow players to hold the ball while pushing once or twice on their wheels. When a player with the ball makes more than two consecutive pushes (without dribbling, passing, or shooting), a traveling violation is called.

Will you need to create specialized equipment? Beep baseball is played with a large softball that beeps so players can track it by hearing, not sight.

Use what you have learned about adaptive sports to come up with your own adapted activity. You might invent a new pastime or a new way of playing an old game that will catch on big!

DISABILITIES AWARENESS   29

ACTIVITIES AND ADAPTATIONS

The Voice of Experience

Whatever activities you enjoy, you can be sure there are many people—with and without disabilities—who like doing the same things. Maybe you belong to a club for people who share your interest, such as an astronomy club or a collectors' group. You might have a friend from the club who has a disability.

Talk with your friend about his or her experiences. Find out what adaptations or adjustments, if any, your friend has made or used to take part in favorite activities or do everyday tasks.

Talk to a Scout who has a disability and learn about his experiences in Scouting. What merit badges has he enjoyed earning? Have any badges presented especially difficult or unsolvable problems? Find out about any adaptive gear or techniques the Scout may have used to achieve his goals in Scouting. Also learn about adaptations or adjustments he may use in his daily life and activities outside Scouting.

DISABILITIES AWARENESS

Alternate Requirements for Boy Scouts

- Scouts with physical or mental disabilities who are unable to complete any or all of the requirements for Tenderfoot, Second Class, or First Class rank may complete alternative requirements if certain criteria are met.
- Scouts with physical or mental disabilities may become Eagle Scouts by earning as many required merit badges for Eagle Scout rank as their abilities permit and qualifying for alternative merit badges for the rest.

To learn more about alternate requirements, see *The Boy Scout Handbook* and the *Boy Scout Requirements* book, and talk to your Scoutmaster.

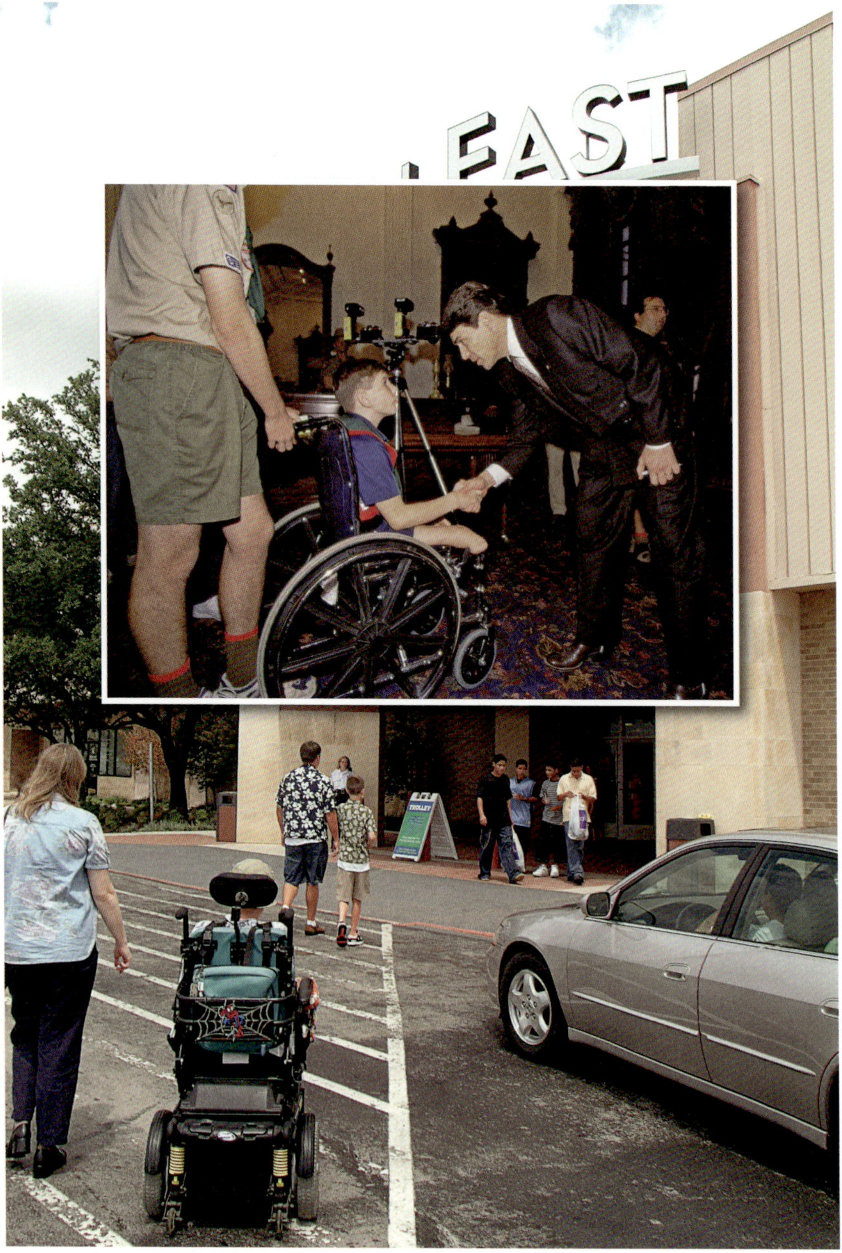
EAST

Accessibility

Curbs or steps without ramps, narrow doorways and aisles, revolving doors and turnstiles, high counters, tight parking spaces with no room to maneuver a wheelchair—any of these can make it impossible for people with disabilities to take part in everyday activities such as shopping in a store, watching a movie in a theater, eating at a restaurant, or even going to school or work.

Next time you are in a public place, look at how accessible (usable) the location is for people with disabilities. Are there:

- Ramps and curb-cuts for wheelchair users?
- Steps that are low and wide enough to be easily climbed by people using crutches or canes?
- Wide doorways?
- Elevators (in buildings of two or more stories)?
- Signs and directions printed in Braille?
- Visual warning signals and directions for people who are deaf?
- Accessible parking spaces wide enough for wheelchairs?
- Accessible restrooms, public telephones, and drinking fountains?
- Tables high enough for a wheelchair user to sit at without banging his or her knees?

ACCESSIBILITY

Some of the accessibility projects suggested in this pamphlet might be done as service projects for achieving the ranks of Star, Life, or Eagle Scout. If you wish to do a project for rank advancement, check with your Scoutmaster to be sure your undertaking meets the standards for leadership service projects.

For requirement 4, you are to give examples of the features of a certain place that make it accessible to people with disabilities, and also some things that could be done to improve upon the site. Some improvements are easy and inexpensive to make. You may be able to increase the accessibility of your school, place of worship, or Scout camp or meeting place.

Here are some simple adaptations you or your patrol might make. Be sure to get permission, and ask for an adult's help if needed.

- Build and install a wooden ramp for wheelchair users.
- Replace round doorknobs (which must be tightly grasped and twisted) with lever handles that are easier for many people with disabilities to use.

34 DISABILITIES AWARENESS

- Move displays so they do not block aisles or hallways.
- Widen a path so people in wheelchairs can use it.
- Remove a fixed seat or bench (one that is bolted to the floor or wall) and replace it with a movable seat that can be moved aside to make room at the table for a person using a wheelchair.
- Make pen and paper available for exchanging written notes with people who are deaf or hard of hearing.
- Make large-print signs using a computer and printer, or by hand-lettering.
- Make signs in Braille using a slate and stylus (a tool used to write Braille much as paper and pencil are used for writing print).
- Read aloud and record on cassettes or CDs the newsletters, brochures, or other printed pieces that give important or useful information about your school, place of worship, or Scout camp. Make the recordings available to visitors or newcomers who are blind or visually impaired.

Recreation Survey

Here is another service idea. Develop a list of local outdoor recreation spots and camping facilities that are accessible to people with disabilities. Create this list by checking with officials at federal, state, and local parks. Ask them the following questions:

- Are the parks barrier-free?
- Are pathways smooth and wide enough for wheelchairs?
- Are drinking fountains and restrooms accessible to wheelchair users?
- Are signs printed in Braille?
- Is any adaptive equipment available for people with disabilities?

When you have compiled your list, neatly type and print it. Distribute photocopies to local organizations for people with disabilities, schools, places of worship, and anywhere else the information will serve people in your community.

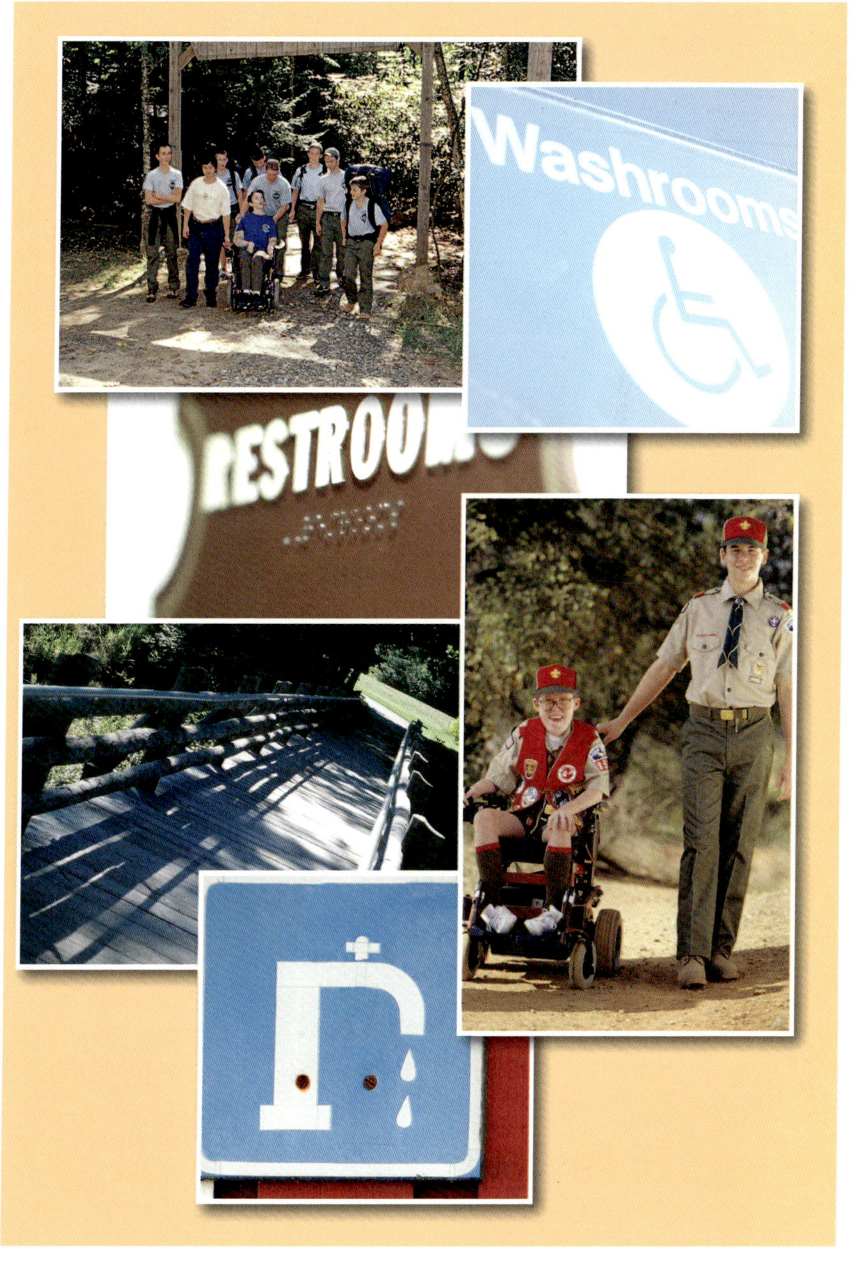
Washrooms

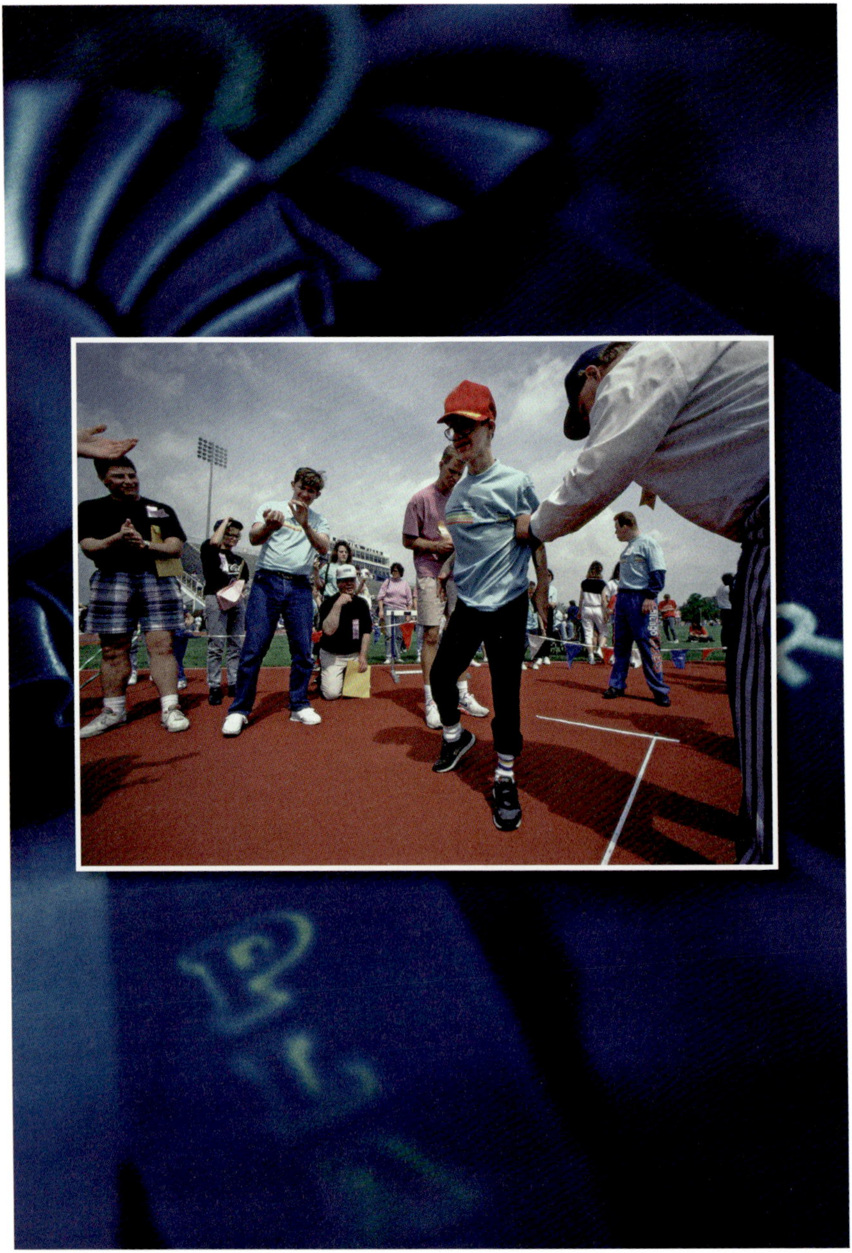

Advocacy, Attitudes, and Awareness

Advocacy means supporting, promoting, or encouraging something. To be an advocate of disabilities awareness means you support and encourage positive attitudes about people who have disabilities. You help strip away the labels so that people can see each other as individuals. You help build bridges of understanding and respect among all people, those with and those without disabilities.

In completing the requirements for the Disabilities Awareness merit badge, you have learned things that you can now teach to others. Use what you have learned to put together a disabilities awareness program that you present (with your counselor's approval) to a Cub Scout pack or other group. Teach the group about person-first language and demonstrate its importance while giving your presentation.

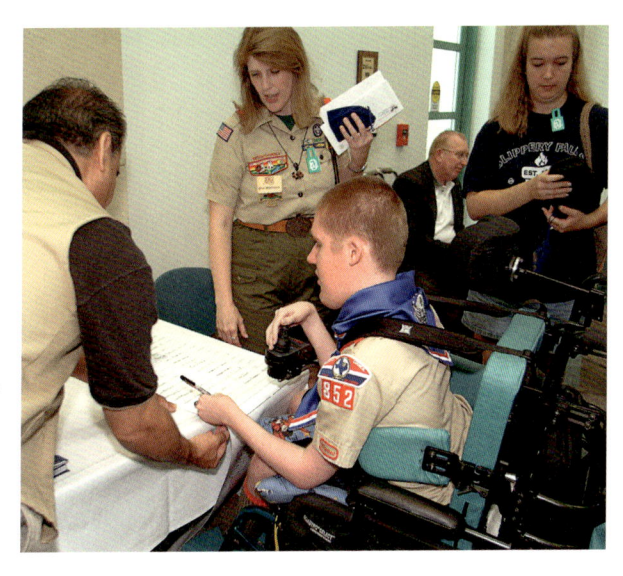

Advocacy, Attitudes, and Awareness

Disabilities come in all sizes, shapes, and forms, just like the people who have them. If you already know something about a specific disability, or would like to learn more about it, you may want to focus on researching and sharing information about that disability and the people who have it. You may choose to give a talk or volunteer with an advocacy program that focuses on the disability of interest.

Here are some possibilities. Add your interest if it is not on this list.

- Amputation
- Arthritis
- Asthma
- Attention-deficit/hyperactivity disorder (ADHD)
- Autism
- Blindness/low vision
- Brain injury
- Cerebral palsy
- Cleft palate
- Cystic fibrosis
- Deafness and hardness of hearing
- Diabetes
- Down syndrome
- Dwarfism
- Epilepsy
- Heart conditions
- Hemophilia
- Learning disabilities
- Leukemia
- Mental disabilities
- Multiple sclerosis
- Muscular dystrophy
- Polio/post-polio
- Sickle-cell anemia
- Speech impairments
- Spina bifida
- Spinal cord injury
- Stroke

ADVOCACY, ATTITUDES, AND AWARENESS

Or, volunteer your time with an education program or advocacy agency in your school or community. The agency you visited for requirement 2 likely will welcome you back as a volunteer. Your school might have education programs with which you could help.

Maybe a group has organized in your area to support a specific issue affecting people with disabilities. You might join with the group (or start one, if none exists) to advocate accessible parking spaces, wheelchair-friendly picnic tables at local parks and playgrounds, or sign-language interpreters for government meetings such as meetings of the city council or school board.

Your counselor might know of, or help you find out about, other volunteer opportunities in your neighborhood. Maybe you can help with programs at a rehabilitation center or camp for children with disabilities. Or be a big brother to a boy or girl who has a disability, giving the child your friendship and help with homework or other needs. Or tutor a student who has learning disabilities, or assist at a Special Olympics competition.

Special Olympics is an international program of games and athletic competition for children and adults who have mental and often physical disabilities. Events are modeled on those of the Olympic Games. Boy Scouts often take part, both as competitors and as helpers. You might organize your patrol or troop to help at a Special Olympics meet.

DISABILITIES AWARENESS   41

ADVOCACY, ATTITUDES, AND AWARENESS

Talk with a physical therapist, occupational therapist, speech therapist, adaptive physical education instructor, recreation program leader, special education teacher, social worker, or other specialist to learn where your efforts are needed.

Hidden Disabilities

Some disabilities are not easy to see. Just because they are not obvious does not make them any less real, however.

Many students have learning disabilities that make it hard for them to acquire, remember, organize, or express thoughts and ideas. People with learning disabilities may have trouble listening, speaking, reading, writing, spelling, visualizing, or doing math despite having average or above-average intelligence. They may do well with one kind of communication, such as writing and reading, and not with another, such as listening. Their coordination, behavior, and interactions with others also may be affected.

Children and young people who are very aggressive, who argue over minor things and have trouble getting along with others, and whose behavior interferes with their education and activities outside of school, may have behavioral disabilities. Young people with these disabilities often do not fully understand how their actions affect others or that their behavior is not appropriate. Not all behavioral disabilities are obvious. Conditions such as depression and anxiety may be hidden.

Kids who have attention-deficit/hyperactivity disorder (AD/HD) may have trouble paying attention and find it hard to get or stay focused on a task or activity. Others with the disorder may be able to pay attention to a task but lose focus because they are hyperactive and impulsive.

Many young people have these kinds of disabilities. You probably know someone who does. If you see yourself in what you have just read, please show your parents this pamphlet and discuss it with them.

Myths and Misconceptions

We are all hurt by mistaken ideas and misunderstandings about people with disabilities and what they can and cannot do. Here are some myths you may hear. Learn the facts so you can share the correct information with others.

Myth: A person with a disability is sick.
Fact: Having a disability is not the same as being sick. Many people with disabilities are in excellent physical condition, healthy, athletic, and strong. Some people who have disabilities also have illnesses, just as some nondisabled people are ill.

Myth: A person with a disability has a poor quality of life or lives a life totally different from people without disabilities.
Fact: Overall, people with disabilities live like anyone else. The attitude that a disability ruins a person's life can be more disabling than the disability itself. People can make adjustments and adaptations that allow them to fully participate, to live full lives, and strive to reach their potential. Although they may do some things differently, depending on the type and extent of the disability, people with disabilities are no different from anyone else.

Myth: People with disabilities deserve special admiration for having the courage and creativity to overcome their disability.
Fact: People with disabilities do not have special virtues. They do not become heroes by adapting to disabilities. Many people with disabilities do not like to be called "brave" or "inspirational." They are just living their lives when they drive to work, shop for groceries, pay their bills, or compete in athletic events.

Myth: Only people in wheelchairs or who use crutches are disabled.
Fact: Many disabilities, such as learning or emotional disabilities, cannot be seen or are not obvious.

Myth: People with disabilities need expensive, high-tech devices for mobility and other assistance.
Fact: Simple, inexpensive tools often are the only help a person with a disability needs to live independently. Assistive devices can be as low-tech as reachers with jaws for grasping objects and bringing them within reach, or grippers for holding eating utensils, toothbrushes, and other small items.

ADVOCACY, ATTITUDES, AND AWARENESS

Myth: People with disabilities can do only light work or only simple, repetitive work.
Fact: People with disabilities work successfully in many different trades, businesses, and professions, having the same responsibilities as nondisabled people. Individuals with disabilities have many different skills to offer, the same as everyone else.

Myth: People with disabilities need to be protected from failing.
Fact: People with disabilities have a right to fail as well as to succeed. Failure is part of the human experience. We all fail sometimes.

Advocacy, Attitudes, and Awareness

Myth: People with disabilities always need help at school or work.
Fact: A person's ability to work or study independently depends on the person's preparation, training, skills, experience, and motivation. These qualities vary among individuals. A person's disability does not necessarily affect his or her qualifications to work unaided or unsupervised.

> **It's the Law.** The Americans With Disabilities Act (ADA) of 1990 is a federal civil rights law that protects people with disabilities from job discrimination. The law also requires that public buildings and transportation systems be accessible to people with disabilities. In addition, the ADA requires telephone companies to provide relay services so that people who are deaf or hard of hearing or who have difficulty speaking can send and receive messages by telephone.

Myth: People who are deaf can easily work in noisy places.
Fact: Loud noises can damage anyone's organs of hearing. People who are deaf should be chosen for positions based on the skills and talents they have, not the disability they have.

Myth: People who are deaf cannot speak.
Fact: Deafness does not affect the vocal cords. People with hearing loss may not hear the sounds they make when they speak. Because they are unable to hear the sound of their voice, some people who are deaf make a conscious choice not to use their voice. Others choose to speak. The age at which the person became deaf also influences speaking ability. Someone who lost his hearing after learning to talk as a child may speak more readily than a person who was born deaf and never heard human speech.

Myth: People who are deaf do not enjoy television shows or movies because they cannot hear.
Fact: Many movies and TV shows are captioned—the words appear on the screen. Performances at theaters may be interpreted into sign language. The type and extent of hearing loss and the age at which the person became deaf also may influence a person's appreciation of vocal art and entertainment.

Myth: All people who are deaf or hard of hearing can read lips.
Fact: Some people lip-read; some do not. Those who do read lips also read facial expressions, gestures, and other body language for help understanding.

Myth: People who are blind have extra-sharp hearing.
Fact: Loss of vision does not affect hearing. However, people who are blind may depend more on their hearing and be more alert to sounds than people who are sighted.

Myth: People who are blind develop a "sixth sense."
Fact: Most people who are blind develop their senses of smell, hearing, taste, and touch more fully, but they do not gain a sixth sense—or a power of perception that most people don't have.

Myth: Employees with disabilities miss more days of work than employees without disabilities.
Fact: Several studies have shown that employees with disabilities are not absent any more often than other employees. In fact, the studies show that, on average, people with disabilities have better attendance rates than their nondisabled coworkers.

Myth: People without disabilities should take care of people with disabilities.
Fact: Anyone may offer help, but most people with disabilities prefer to be self-sufficient and responsible for themselves when possible.

= ADVOCACY, ATTITUDES, AND AWARENESS

Changing Attitudes

To wrap up your work on the Disabilities Awareness merit badge, discuss with your counselor your own attitudes about people with disabilities. Has your work on this badge given you insight or changed your outlook? Tell your counselor how you intend to use proper disability etiquette, show positive attitudes, and encourage them in others.

You have seen that people with disabilities are all individuals. Each person has talents, abilities, feelings, likes, dislikes, wants, and needs. Each person has the right to be treated respectfully, as an individual.

You also have learned that people with disabilities are people first. And maybe you have realized that all people are more alike than different. People are people. Individual variations aside, we are all much the same.

> "If you inquire what the people are like here, I must answer, 'The same as everywhere.'"
> —Johann Wolfgang van Goethe (1749–1832), German poet and novelist

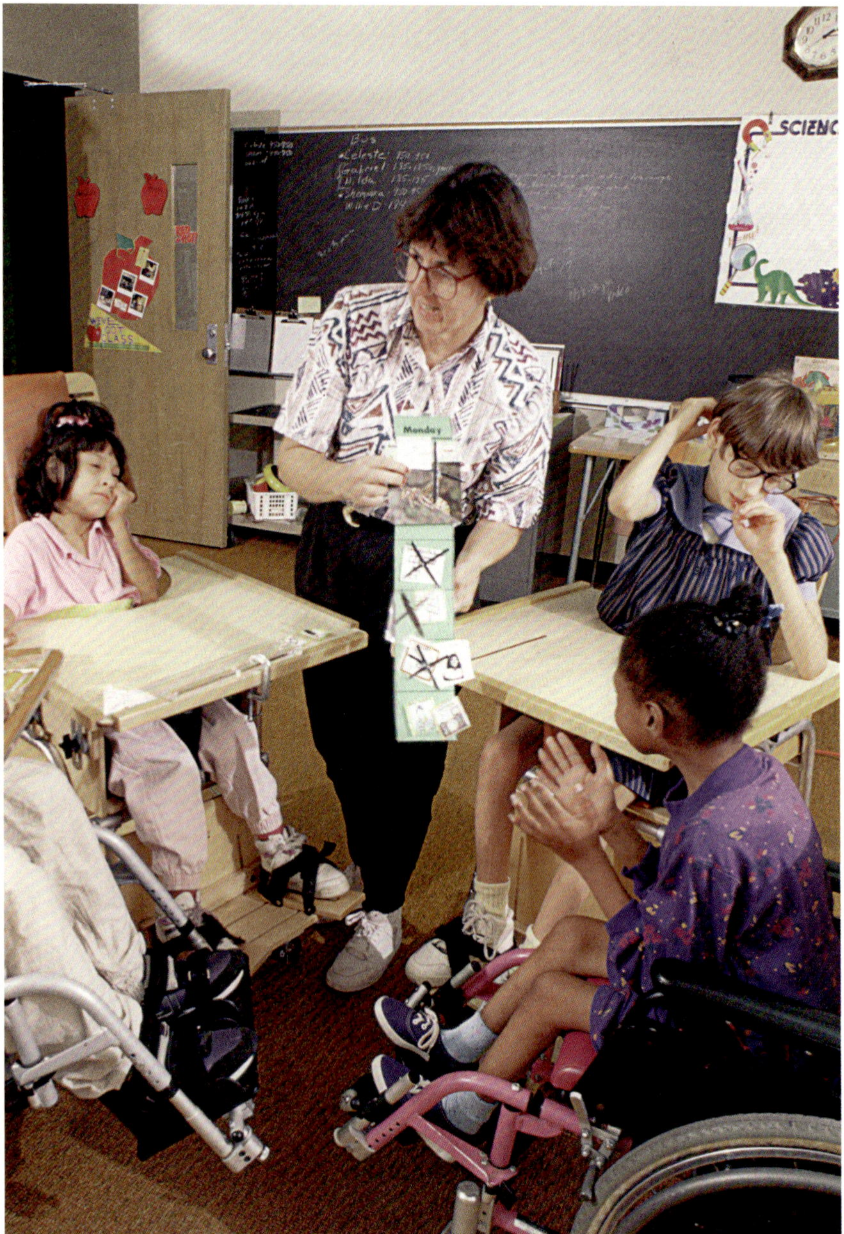
SCIENC
Monday

Career Opportunities

Many types of specialists work with people who have disabilities. Some of the careers you might pursue are described here. Your merit badge counselor may know of other positions in this field that might appeal to you.

Occupational therapists teach skills to help people with disabilities do the things they need to do. Occupational therapists work in hospitals, clinics, rehabilitation centers, mental health centers, schools, nursing homes, child-care centers, and in some cases patients' private homes. A bachelor's or master's degree in occupational therapy is required. College programs include courses in biology, psychology, and occupational therapy theory and practice.

> In occupational therapy, the focus is on practical activities and the skills of daily life. For example, someone who has lost both legs may learn how to drive a specially equipped car. A person who uses a wheelchair might be taught how to maneuver in the kitchen and cook while seated. To help a child with a learning disability learn to recognize shapes or colors, an occupational therapist might have the child play games or do crafts that require matching items of different shapes, sizes, and colors.

If a career in this field interests you, you should begin early to get the background needed. In school, take biology, physical science, language, and physical education classes. Get an after-school job or volunteer with an agency or organization that serves people who have disabilities.

Career Opportunities

Physical therapists use treatments of heat, cold, light, sound, water, and exercise to treat diseases or injuries, build stamina and strength, and restore function to parts of the body. Physical therapy can help prevent, reduce, or relieve conditions that affect a person's physical abilities. Physical therapists work in the same types of places as occupational therapists. Most physical therapists have a master's degree, but a growing number of them have a doctor of physical therapy (DPT) degree. Physical therapy studies include courses in anatomy, physiology, psychology, and therapeutic exercise. In the United States, physical therapists must be licensed before they may practice.

Special education teachers help children with disabilities learn to the fullest of their abilities. These teachers may work in schools, homes, hospitals, and institutions. They help students get mainstreamed into regular education classes and succeed in life after leaving school. This career field requires at least a bachelor's degree and teaching credential.

Audiologists are trained to detect and diagnose hearing problems. An audiologist uses an instrument called an audiometer to test a person's hearing. An audiologist also may give behavioral tests to find out how a person reacts to various sounds and vibrations. Most audiologists have at least a master's degree and many have a doctorate degree. College

= CAREER OPPORTUNITIES

programs in audiology include courses in hearing, speech, and language. Audiologists may work in schools, hospitals, clinics, private offices, and community speech and hearing centers. To practice audiology in the United States, a person usually needs a certificate or license.

Speech therapists (also called speech-language pathologists or speech clinicians) work with children and adults who have speech disorders that interfere with communication or make people self-conscious when they talk. Most speech therapists have at least a master's degree. They work in schools, hospitals, speech clinics, specialized speech and hearing centers, or private practice. College students interested in speech therapy take courses in biology, linguistics, psychology, physics, and speech correction.

Psychologists study mental processes and behavior and how people relate to one another and to the world around them. Many psychologists treat emotional problems and serve as counselors or therapists in schools, hospitals, rehabilitation centers, clinics, mental health centers, or private practice. Some positions in psychology require only a bachelor's or master's degree, but most require a doctorate degree. A doctorate usually takes four or more years of study beyond a bachelor's degree. In addition, most people who plan to become clinical psychologists work at least a year as an intern, treating patients under the supervision of experienced psychologists.

Some of the more common speech disorders include stuttering, lisping, slurred speech, delayed speech and slow language development, the inability to make certain sounds, and the partial or total inability to speak or understand language.

DISABILITIES AWARENESS   51

Career Opportunities

An intern is an advanced student or a graduate who gets practical, on-the-job experience under the supervision of someone more expert.

Psychology is similar to a medical field called *psychiatry*. Psychologists may or may not specialize in treating mental disorders. Psychiatrists, however, are medical doctors whose field is the treatment of mental disorders. A psychiatrist might work in a mental health center, in a mental institution, or in private practice.

Other *physicians* working with people who have disabilities are specially trained in physical medicine and rehabilitation. Many hospitals have a rehabilitation department that provides patients with physical and occupational therapy. Treatment is usually carried out by a team of specialists that may include physicians, nurses, psychologists, social workers, speech pathologists, and various other therapists.

Vocational rehabilitation programs prepare people with physical or mental disabilities to hold jobs. There are three main areas: rehabilitation counseling, vocational evaluation, and placement. A *rehabilitation counselor* advises people with

= CAREER OPPORTUNITIES

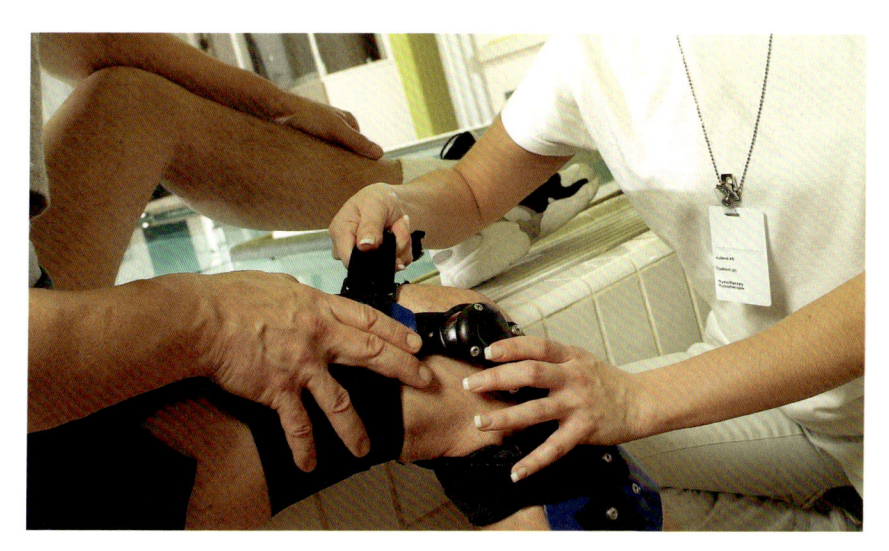

disabilities about the type of training they may need or the tasks they can perform. A *vocational evaluator* gives tests to discover a person's abilities and interests and determine what specific position or field of training will suit the person. A *placement specialist* helps people put their interests and skills to use. Careers in vocational rehabilitation generally require at least a bachelor's degree; most require a master's degree. College students majoring in rehabilitation take courses in counseling, human relations, psychology, statistics, and testing, and complete an internship. Vocational rehabilitation specialists may work for hospitals and rehabilitation centers or for state-operated vocational rehab programs and programs serving military veterans with disabilities.

Disabilities Awareness Resources

Scouting Literature

Architecture, Athletics, Citizenship in the Community, Citizenship in the Nation, Citizenship in the World, Communications, Computers, Engineering, First Aid, Medicine, Public Speaking, and *Sports* merit badge pamphlets

> Visit the Boy Scouts of America's official retail Web site at *http://www.scoutstuff.org* for a complete listing of all merit badge pamphlets and other helpful Scouting materials and supplies.

Boys' Life magazine in Braille. National Library Service for the Blind and Physically Handicapped, Library of Congress, Washington DC. Telephone: 202-707-5104

Recordings of the *Boy Scout Handbook* and various merit badge pamphlets. Recordings for the Blind and Dyslexic. Toll-free telephone: 800-221-4792

Boy Scout Handbook in Braille. The Lighthouse of Houston. Telephone: 713-527-9561

Boy Scout Handbook in large print. Boy Scout Division. Telephone: 972-580-2439

BSA merit badge pamphlets in Braille. National Braille Association. Telephone: 716-427-8260

Ad Altare Dei Participant Manuals in Braille can be rented from the BSA Relationships Division at the national office in Irving, Texas, telephone: 972-580-2114. There is a minimal rental cost of $2 each, plus shipping and a security deposit of $25 to be refunded when texts are returned within a six-month time frame.

Scouts With Disabilities and Special Needs fact sheet, No. 02-508

Scouting for Youth With Emotional Disabilities, No. 32998D

Scouting for Youth With Physical Disabilities, No. 33057D

Scouting for Youth With Mental Retardation, No. 33059C

Scouting for Youth Who Are Deaf, No. 33061B

Scouting for the Blind and Visually Impaired, No. 33063D

Scouting for Youth With Learning Disabilities, No. 33065B

Books

Fiction

Many of these novels are classics available in several editions and formats including audio, and some are available in large print.

Burnett, Frances Hodgson. *The Secret Garden.* HarperCollins, 1987. Colin behaves like a spoiled and incurable invalid until his orphaned cousin Mary comes to live in their lonely house on the Yorkshire moors. The two discover the mysteries and magic of a locked garden, and gradually transform the garden and themselves.

Byars, Betsy. *The Summer of the Swans.* Penguin Putnam Books, 2004. A teenager gains new insight into herself and her family when her brother with mental retardation goes missing.

De Angeli, Marguerite. *The Door in the Wall.* Yearling Books, 1990. In 14th-century England, a boy with physical disabilities proves his courage.

Dorris, Michael. *Sees Behind Trees.* Disney Press, 1997. An American Indian boy with a special gift to "see" beyond his limited eyesight journeys with an old warrior to a land of mystery and beauty.

Flegg, Aubrey. *The Cinnamon Tree: A Novel Set in Africa.* O'Brien Press, 2001. When a land mine explodes beneath her, Yola Abonda is thrown violently into a new life. She must learn to walk again after the amputation of her leg.

Konigsburg, E. L. *The View from Saturday.* Aladdin Paperbacks, 1998. Four students with their own individual stories develop a special bond and attract the attention of their teacher, a paraplegic, who chooses them to represent their sixth-grade class in the Academic Bowl competition.

Martin, Ann M. *A Corner of the Universe.* Scholastic, 2002. Now that Uncle Adam's "school"—an institution for people with mental disabilities—is closing, 12-year-old Hattie's family must deal with a childlike young man whose existence they have denied for years.

Philbrick, Rodman. *Freak the Mighty.* Scholastic Signature, 2001. At the beginning of eighth grade, Max, who has learning disabilities and a mighty physique, and his new friend Freak, who was born with a condition that affects his body but not his brilliant mind, find that when they unite to become "Freak the Mighty" they make a powerful team.

Taylor, Theodore. *The Cay.* Yearling Books, 2002. When the freighter on which they are traveling is torpedoed by a German submarine during World War II, an adolescent white boy, blinded by a blow on the head, and an old African American man are stranded on a tiny island where the boy gains a new kind of vision.

Winkler, Henry. *Niagara Falls, or Does It?* Turtleback Books, 2003. Inspired by his own experiences with undiagnosed dyslexia, actor/director Henry Winkler presents "Hank Zipzer: The Mostly True Confessions of the World's Best Underachiever," a series about the adventures of a fourth-grader with learning differences. In this first book of the series, Hank is supposed to write an essay on how he spent the summer, but decides instead to "show" what he did.

Nonfiction

Aaseng, Nathan. *Multiple Sclerosis.* Franklin Watts, 2000. Describes the symptoms, effects, and treatments of the neurological disease known as MS and tells the stories of several well-known people who have this disease.

Burnett, Gail Lemley. *Muscular Dystrophy.* Enslow Publishers, 2000. Discusses the cause, symptoms, and treatment of muscular dystrophy and examines research into treatment and a possible cure.

Clayton, Lawrence, and Jaydene Morrison. *Coping with a Learning Disability.* Hazelden Publishing & Educational Services, 1999. Guide for young adults in learning how to cope with the difficulties that come with having a learning disability.

Corman, Richard. *I Am Proud: The Athletes of Special Olympics.* Barnes & Noble Books, 2003. Portrays the athletes' dignity, grace, and joy in competition and brings fresh perspective to a group of people too often defined by their perceived disabilities.

Cummings, Rhoda Woods, and Gary L. Fisher. *The Survival Guide for Teenagers With LD: Learning Differences.* Free Spirit Publishing, 1993. A handbook with a positive outlook for teenagers who have learning differences on how to make friends, set goals, start a career, and manage other day-to-day pursuits.

Dudley, Mark Edward. *Epilepsy.* Enslow Publishers, 2001. Discusses the causes, diagnosis, and treatment of epilepsy; the types of seizures; and challenges of living with this disease.

Flodin, Mickey. *Signing for Kids: The Fun Way for Anyone to Learn American Sign Language.* Perigee Books, 1991. An introduction to the expressive language used by many deaf people to speak with their hands.

Freedman, Russell. *Out of Darkness: The Story of Louis Braille.* Clarion Books, 1999. A biography of the 19th-century Frenchman who, having himself been blinded at age 3, developed a system of raised dots on paper that enabled those who are blind to read and write.

Gold, John Coopersmith. *Cerebral Palsy.* Enslow Publishers, 2001. Readers learn what life is like with cerebral palsy in this sensitive, scientific discussion of an incurable disorder that strikes about two in 1,000 infants yearly in the United States.

Kent, Deborah, and Kathryn A. Quinlan. *Extraordinary People With Disabilities.* Children's Press, 1997. Collection of biographies of 48 famous people who have made great accomplishments despite their disability.

Meyer, Donald, ed. *Views From Our Shoes: Growing Up With a Brother or Sister With Special Needs.* Woodbine House, 1997. Kids ranging in age from 4 to 18 share their experiences as the brother or sister of someone with a disability, including autism, cerebral palsy, development delays, attention deficit disorder, hydrocephalus, visual and hearing impairments, and Down and Tourette syndromes.

Oleksy, Walter G. *Christopher Reeve.* Greenhaven Press, 2000. Discusses the personal life, acting career, and life-altering accident of the actor known for his role as Superman and for his efforts on behalf of people with spinal cord injuries.

Rogers, Dale Evans. *Angel Unaware.* Revell, 1992. The story of a child born with Down syndrome—Robin Elizabeth Rogers, daughter of celebrities Roy Rogers and Dale Evans. This book sold more than 500,000 copies when first published in 1953.

Stern, Judith, and Uzi Ben-Ami. *Many Ways to Learn: Young People's Guide to Learning Disabilities.* Magination Press, 1996. Describes different kinds of learning disabilities, explains that children with learning disabilities have average (if not above-average) intelligence, and discusses the many things kids can do to reach their goals.

Weihenmayer, Erik. *Touch the Top of the World: A Blind Man's Journey to Climb Farther Than the Eye Can See.* Plume Books, 2002. An adventure-packed memoir in which the author recalls rebelling against becoming blind by age 15, acquiring a passion for mountain climbing, and developing the character traits that enabled him to succeed. His experiences remind readers of what the blind and the sighted have in common.

Williams, Donna. *Nobody Nowhere: The Extraordinary Autobiography of an Autistic.* Perennial, 1994. Takes readers on a journey into the mind of a person who has autism, giving an insider's view of a little-understood condition and destroying many myths and misconceptions.

Woodyard, Shawn, John Bradford, and Elizabeth Oakes. *Resources for People With Disabilities: A National Directory,* 2nd ed. Ferguson Publishing Company, 1998. The "yellow pages" for people with disabilities, this two-volume set provides information about resources pertaining to advocacy, assistive technology, organizations and associations, rehabilitation, and state programs, to name just a few.

Disabilities Awareness Resources

Organizations and Web Sites

American Academy of Physical Medicine and Rehabilitation
330 North Wabash Ave., Suite 2500
Chicago, IL 60611-7617
Telephone: 312-464-9700
Web site: *http://www.aapmr.org*

American Association of People With Disabilities
1629 K St. NW, Suite 503
Washington, DC 20006
Toll-free telephone (voice and TTY): 800-840-8844
Web site: *http://www.aapd-dc.org*

American Association on Intellectual and Developmental Disabilities
444 N. Capitol St. NW, Suite 846
Washington, DC 20001-1512
Toll-free telephone: 800-424-3688
Web site: *http://www.aaidd.org*

American Council of the Blind
1155 15th St. NW, Suite 1004
Washington, DC 20005
Toll-free telephone: 800-424-8666
Web site: *http://www.acb.org*

American Foundation for the Blind
11 Penn Plaza, Suite 300
New York, NY 10001
Toll-free telephone: 800-232-5463
Web site: *http://www.afb.org*

American Printing House for the Blind
P.O. Box 6085
Louisville, KY 40206-0085
Telephone: 502-895-2405
Web site: *http://www.aph.org*

American Speech-Language-Hearing Association
10801 Rockville Pike
Rockville, MD 20852
Telephone: 800-638-8255
Web site: *http://www.asha.org*

The Arc of the United States
1010 Wayne Ave., Suite 650
Silver Spring, MD 20910
Telephone: 301-565-3842
Web site: *http://www.thearc.org*

Attention Deficit Disorder Association
15000 Commerce Pkwy., Suite C
Mount Lauel, NJ 08054
Telephone: 856-439-9099
Web site: *http://www.add.org*

Autism Society of America
7910 Woodmont Ave., Suite 300
Bethesda, MD 20814-3067
Toll-free telephone: 800-328-8476
Web site: *http://www.autism-society.org*

Brain Injury Association of America
1608 Spring Hill Road, Suite 110
Vienna, VA 22182
Telephone: 703-761-0750
Web site: *http://www.biausa.org*

Children and Adults With Attention-Deficit/Hyperactivity Disorder
8181 Professional Place, Suite 150
Landover, MD 20785
National Resource Center on AD/HD, toll-free telephone: 800-233-4050
Web site: *http://www.chadd.org*

DisabilityInfo.gov
Web site: *http://www.disabilityinfo.gov*

Disability Is Natural
BraveHeart Press
P.O. Box 7245
Woodland Park, CO 80863
Toll-free telephone: 866-948-2222
Web site: *http://www.disabilityisnatural.com*

Disabilities Awareness Resources

Disabled American Veterans
P.O. Box 14301
Cincinnati, OH 45250-0301
Telephone: 859-441-7300
Web site: *http://www.dav.org*

Disabled Sports USA
451 Hungerford Drive, Suite 100
Rockville, MD 20850
Telephone: 301-217-0960
Web site: *http://www.dsusa.org*

Easter Seals
230 W. Monroe St., Suite 1800
Chicago, IL 60606
Toll-free telephone: 800-221-6827
TTY: 312-726-4258
Web site: *http://www.easterseals.com*

Goodwill Industries International Inc.
15810 Indianola Drive
Rockville, MD 20855
Toll-free telephone: 800-741-0186
Web site: *http://www.goodwill.org*

Guide Dogs for the Blind
P.O. Box 151200
San Rafael, CA 94915-1200
Toll-free telephone: 800-295-4050
Web site: *http://www.guidedogs.com*

Helping Hands
541 Cambridge St.
Boston, MA 02134-2023
Telephone: 617-787-4419
Web site: *http://www.helping handmonkeys.org/*

International Dyslexia Association
40 York Road, Fourth Floor
Baltimore, MD 21204
Telephone: 410-296-0232
Web site: *http://www.interdys.org*

International Paralympic Committee
U.S. Paralympics
One Olympic Plaza
Colorado Springs, CO 80909
Telephone: 719-866-2035
Web site: *http://www.paralympic.org*

Kids on the Block Inc.
9385-C Gerwig Lane
Columbia, MD 21046
Toll-free telephone: 800-368-5437
Web site: *http://www.kotb.com*

Learning Disabilities Association of America
4156 Library Road
Pittsburgh, PA 15234-1349
Telephone: 412-341-1515
Web site: *http://www.ldanatl.org*

Mental Health Association
2000 N. Beauregard St., Sixth Floor
Alexandria, VA 22311
Toll-free telephone: 800-969-6642
TTY: 800-433-5959
Web site: *http://www.nmha.org*

Muscular Dystrophy Association—USA
National Headquarters
3300 East Sunrise Drive
Tucson, AZ 85718
Toll-free telephone: 800-344-4863
Web site: *http://www.mdausa.org*

National Association of the Deaf
8630 Fenton St., Suite 820
Silver Spring, MD 20910-3819
Telephone: 301-587-1788
TTY: 301-587-1789
Web site: *http://www.nad.org*

National Center for Learning Disabilities
381 Park Ave. South, Suite 1401
New York, NY 10016
Toll-free telephone: 888-575-7373
Web site: *http://www.ncld.org*

Disabilities Awareness Resources

The National Center on Physical Activity and Disability
1640 W. Roosevelt Road
Chicago, IL 60608-6904
Toll-free telephone (voice and TTY): 800-900-8086
Web site: http://www.ncpad.org

National Disability Sports Alliance
25 W. Independence Way
Kingston, RI 02882
Telephone: 401-792-7130
Web site: http://www.ndsaonline.org

National Dissemination Center for Children With Disabilities
P.O. Box 1492
Washington, DC 20013
Toll-free telephone (voice/TTY): 800-695-0285
Web site: http://www.nichcy.org

National Down Syndrome Society
666 Broadway
New York, NY 10012
Toll-free telephone: 800-221-4602
Web site: http://www.ndss.org

National Federation of the Blind
1800 Johnson St.
Baltimore, MD 21230
Telephone: 410-659-9314
Web site: http://www.nfb.org

National Library Service for the Blind and Physically Handicapped
Library of Congress
Washington, DC 20542
Toll-free telephone: 888-657-7323
TDD: 202-707-0744
Web site: http://www.loc.gov/nls

National Multiple Sclerosis Society
733 Third Ave., Third Floor
New York, NY 10017
Toll-free telephone: 800-344-4867
Web site: http://www.nationalmssociety.org

National Organization on Disability
910 16th St. NW, Suite 600
Washington, DC 20006
Telephone: 202-293-5960
TTY: 202-293-5968
Web site: http://www.nod.org

National Rehabilitation Information Center
8201 Corporate Drive, Suite 600
Landover, MD 20785
Toll-free telephone: 800-346-2742
TTY: 301-459-5984
Web site: http://www.naric.com

Special Olympics International
1133 19th St. NW
Washington, DC 20036
Telephone: 202-628-3630
Web site: http://www.specialolympics.org

United Cerebral Palsy
1660 L St. NW, Suite 700
Washington, DC 20036
Toll-free telephone: 800-872-5827
Web site: http://www.ucp.org

United States Association of Blind Athletes
33 N. Institute St.
Colorado Springs, CO 80903
Telephone: 719-630-0422
Web site: http://www.usaba.org

USA Deaf Sports Federation
102 N. Krohn Place
Sioux Falls, SD 57103-1800
Telephone: 605-367-5760
TTY: 605-367-5761
Web site: http://www.usadsf.org

Wheelchair Sports, USA
1236 Jungermann Road, Suite A
St. Peters, MO 63376
Telephone: 515-833-2450
Web site: http://www.wsusa.org

Acknowledgments

The Boy Scouts of America thanks the following individuals, who were generous with their knowledge and time in assisting us with this new edition of the *Disabilities Awareness* merit badge pamphlet.

- Sara Qureshi, director, Program Support, The Kids on the Block
- Chris Privett, communications director, The Arc of the United States
- Doug Hind, manager, Special Curriculum, The Church of Jesus Christ of Latter-day Saints
- Dale McClellan, administrative assistant to the Young Men general presidency, The Church of Jesus Christ of Latter-day Saints

Photo and Illustration Credits

Franklin D. Roosevelt Presidential Library/Margaret Suckley, courtesy—page 11 *(Roosevelt)*

©Guide Dogs for the Blind Inc., courtesy—cover *(guide dog);* pages 18 and 20–21 *(both)*

Harris Communications, courtesy—cover *(teletypewriter);* page 24 *(top)*

©Jupiterimages.com—cover *(wheelchair, prosthetic leg);* pages 4, 23 *(top)*, 34 *(bottom)*, 35, 37 *(all except two Scout photos),* and 50–53 *(all)*

Library of Congress Prints and Photographs Division, courtesy—page 11 *(Tubman)*

National Sports Center for the Disabled, courtesy—cover *(skier)*

©Photos.com—pages 23 *(bottom)*, 38 *(background)*, 40, and 47

Randall Anderson/Rossmiller Photography, courtesy—page 11 *(Waddell)*

Rogers & Cowan, courtesy—page 11 *(Glover)*

San Diego Hall of Champions, courtesy—page 11 *(Larson)*

Charlie L. Soap, courtesy—page 11 *(Mankiller)*

Wikipedia.org, courtesy—cover *(hearing aid);* page 27 *(top)*

Wikipedia.org/Sarah Chester, courtesy—cover *(folding cane)*

All other photos and illustrations not mentioned above are the property of or are protected by the Boy Scouts of America.

Dan Bryant—cover *(van);* pages 12, 32 *(background)*, 33, 39, and 46

Tom Copeland Jr.—page 10

Ernest Doclar—page 27 *(bottom)*

Randy Piland—pages 6 *(foreground)*, 28, 31, and 36

Steve Seeger—page 26

Emery Shepard—page 6 *(background)*

Notes

Notes

Notes